Don't Sweat the Small Stuff
. . .and it's all small stuff

A 1999 Date Book to Keep the
Little Things from Taking Over Your Life

Don't Sweat the Small Stuff
. . .and it's all small stuff

A 1999 Date Book to Keep the Little Things from Taking Over Your Life

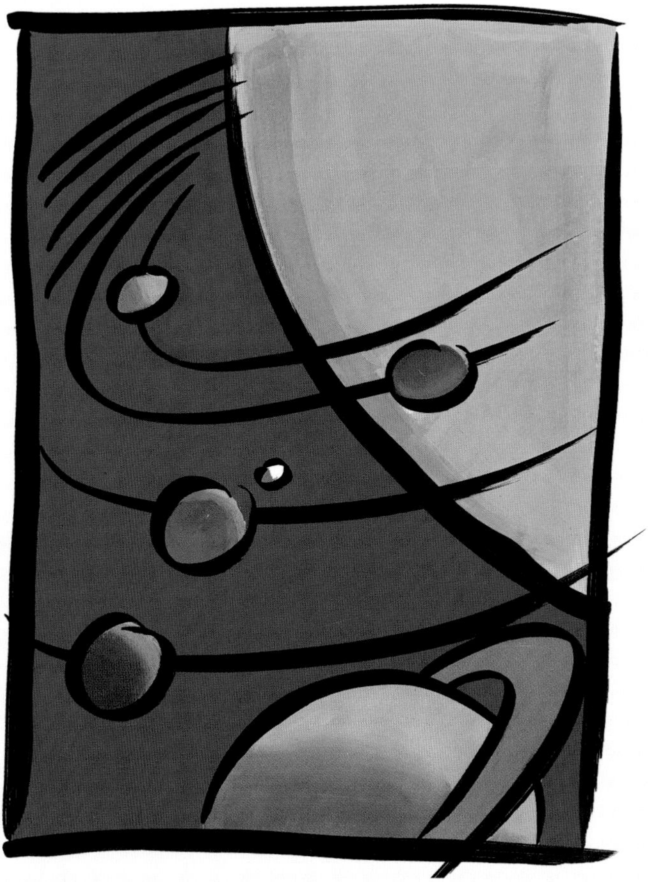

Richard Carlson, PH.D.

HYPERION
New York

Designed by Claudyne Bianco Bedell

Illustrations by Julie Johnson

First Edition

ISBN 0-7868-8346-4

10 9 8 7 6 5 4 3 2 1

Don't Sweat the Small Stuff
. . .and it's all small stuff

A 1999 Date Book to Keep the Little Things from Taking Over Your Life

January

BECOME AN EARLY RISER

Whenever we're dealing with bad news, a difficult person, or a disappointment of some kind, most of us get into certain habits, ways of reacting to life—particularly adversity—that don't serve us very well. We overreact, blow things out of proportion, hold on too tightly, and focus on the negative aspects of life. When we are immobilized by little things—when we are irritated, annoyed, and easily bothered—our (over-) reactions not only make us frustrated but actually get in the way of getting what we want.

December - January

SUNDAY 27

MONDAY 28

TUESDAY 29

WEDNESDAY 30

THURSDAY 31

FRIDAY 1

NEW YEAR'S DAY

SATURDAY 2

DECEMBER

S	M	T	W	T	F	S
		1	2	3	4	5
6	7	8	9	10	11	12
13	14	15	16	17	18	19
20	21	22	23	24	25	26
27	28	29	30	31		

FEBRUARY

S	M	T	W	T	F	S
	1	2	3	4	5	6
7	8	9	10	11	12	13
14	15	16	17	18	19	20
21	22	23	24	25	26	27
28						

When you "don't sweat the small stuff," your life won't be perfect, but you will learn to accept what life has to offer with far less resistance. As we learn in the Zen philosophy, when you learn to "let go" of problems instead of resisting with all your might, your life will begin to flow. You will, as the serenity prayer suggests, "Change the things that can be changed, accept those that cannot, and have the wisdom to know the difference."

January

SUNDAY 3

MONDAY 4

TUESDAY 5

WEDNESDAY 6

THURSDAY 7

FRIDAY 8

SATURDAY 9

DECEMBER

S	M	T	W	T	F	S
		1	2	3	4	5
6	7	8	9	10	11	12
13	14	15	16	17	18	19
20	21	22	23	24	25	26
27	28	29	30	31		

FEBRUARY

S	M	T	W	T	F	S
	1	2	3	4	5	6
7	8	9	10	11	12	13
14	15	16	17	18	19	20
21	22	23	24	25	26	27
28						

Often we allow ourselves to get all worked up about things that, upon closer examination, aren't really that big a deal. We focus on little problems and concerns and blow them way out of proportion. A stranger, for example, might cut in front of us in traffic. Rather than let it go, and go on with our day, we convince ourselves that we are justified in our anger. We play out an imaginary confrontation in our mind. Many of us might even tell someone else about the incident later on rather than simply let it go.

January

SUNDAY 10

MONDAY 11

TUESDAY 12

WEDNESDAY 13

THURSDAY 14

FRIDAY 15

SATURDAY 16

DECEMBER

S	M	T	W	T	F	S
		1	2	3	4	5
6	7	8	9	10	11	12
13	14	15	16	17	18	19
20	21	22	23	24	25	26
27	28	29	30	31		

FEBRUARY

S	M	T	W	T	F	S
	1	2	3	4	5	6
7	8	9	10	11	12	13
14	15	16	17	18	19	20
21	22	23	24	25	26	27
28						

I've yet to meet an absolute perfectionist whose life was filled with inner peace. The need for perfection and the desire for inner tranquility conflict with each other. Whenever we are attached to having something a certain way, better than it already is, we are, almost by definition, engaged in a losing battle. Rather than being content and grateful for what we have, we are focused on what's wrong with something and our need to fix it. When we are zeroed in on what's wrong, it implies that we are dissatisfied, discontent.

January

SUNDAY 17

MONDAY 18

MARTIN LUTHER KING JR. DAY

TUESDAY 19

WEDNESDAY 20

THURSDAY 21

FRIDAY 22

SATURDAY 23

DECEMBER

S	M	T	W	T	F	S
		1	2	3	4	5
6	7	8	9	10	11	12
13	14	15	16	17	18	19
20	21	22	23	24	25	26
27	28	29	30	31		

FEBRUARY

S	M	T	W	T	F	S
	1	2	3	4	5	6
7	8	9	10	11	12	13
14	15	16	17	18	19	20
21	22	23	24	25	26	27
28						

One of the major reasons so many of us remain hurried, frightened, and competitive, and continue to live life as if it were one giant emergency, is our fear that if we were to become more peaceful and loving, we would suddenly stop achieving our goals. We would become lazy and apathetic.

January

SUNDAY 24

MONDAY 25

TUESDAY 26

WEDNESDAY 27

THURSDAY 28

FRIDAY 29

SATURDAY 30

DECEMBER

S	M	T	W	T	F	S
		1	2	3	4	5
6	7	8	9	10	11	12
13	14	15	16	17	18	19
20	21	22	23	24	25	26
27	28	29	30	31		

FEBRUARY

S	M	T	W	T	F	S
	1	2	3	4	5	6
7	8	9	10	11	12	13
14	15	16	17	18	19	20
21	22	23	24	25	26	27
28						

February

FILL YOUR LIFE WITH LOVE

A powerful technique for becoming more peaceful is to be aware of how quickly your negative and insecure thinking can spiral out of control. Have you ever noticed how uptight you feel when you're caught up in your thinking? And, to top it off, the more absorbed you get in the details of whatever is upsetting you, the worse you feel. One thought leads to another, and yet another, until at some point, you become incredibly agitated.

The solution is to notice what's happening in your head before your thoughts have a chance to build any momentum. The sooner you catch yourself in the act of building your mental snowball, the easier it is to stop. In our example here, you might notice your snowball thinking right when you start running through the list of what you have to do the next day. Then, instead of obsessing on your upcoming day, you say to yourself, "Whew, there I go again," and consciously nip it in the bud.

January - February

SUNDAY 31

MONDAY 1

TUESDAY 2

GROUNDHOG DAY

WEDNESDAY 3

THURSDAY 4

FRIDAY 5

SATURDAY 6

JANUARY

S	M	T	W	T	F	S
					1	2
3	4	5	6	7	8	9
10	11	12	13	14	15	16
17	18	19	20	21	22	23
24	25	26	27	28	29	30
31						

MARCH

S	M	T	W	T	F	S
	1	2	3	4	5	6
7	8	9	10	11	12	13
14	15	16	17	18	19	20
21	22	23	24	25	26	27
28	29	30	31			

Nothing helps us build our perspective more than developing compassion for others. Compassion is a sympathetic feeling. It involves the willingness to put yourself in someone else's shoes, to take the focus off yourself and to imagine what it's like to be in someone else's predicament, and simultaneously, to feel love for that person.

February

SUNDAY 7

MONDAY 8

TUESDAY 9

WEDNESDAY 10

THURSDAY 11

FRIDAY 12

LINCOLN'S BIRTHDAY

SATURDAY 13

JANUARY

S	M	T	W	T	F	S
					1	2
3	4	5	6	7	8	9
10	11	12	13	14	15	16
17	18	19	20	21	22	23
24	25	26	27	28	29	30
31						

MARCH

S	M	T	W	T	F	S
	1	2	3	4	5	6
7	8	9	10	11	12	13
14	15	16	17	18	19	20
21	22	23	24	25	26	27
28	29	30	31			

The nature of your "in basket" is that it's meant to have items to be completed in it—it's not meant to be empty. There will always be phone calls that need to be made, projects to complete, and work to be done. In fact, it can be argued that a full "in basket" is essential for success. It means your time is in demand!

February

SUNDAY 14

VALENTINE'S DAY

MONDAY 15

PRESIDENTS' DAY

TUESDAY 16

WEDNESDAY 17

CHINESE NEW YEAR
ASH WEDNESDAY

THURSDAY 18

FRIDAY 19

SATURDAY 20

JANUARY

S	M	T	W	T	F	S
					1	2
3	4	5	6	7	8	9
10	11	12	13	14	15	16
17	18	19	20	21	22	23
24	25	26	27	28	29	30
31						

MARCH

S	M	T	W	T	F	S
	1	2	3	4	5	6
7	8	9	10	11	12	13
14	15	16	17	18	19	20
21	22	23	24	25	26	27
28	29	30	31			

While all acts of kindness are inherently wonderful, there is something even more magical about doing something thoughtful but mentioning it to no one, ever. You always feel good when you give to others. Rather than diluting the positive feelings by telling others about your own kindness, by keeping it to yourself you get to retain all the positive feelings.

February

SUNDAY 21

MONDAY 22

WASHINGTON'S BIRTHDAY

TUESDAY 23

WEDNESDAY 24

THURSDAY 25

FRIDAY 26

SATURDAY 27

JANUARY

S	M	T	W	T	F	S
					1	2
3	4	5	6	7	8	9
10	11	12	13	14	15	16
17	18	19	20	21	22	23
24	25	26	27	28	29	30
31						

MARCH

S	M	T	W	T	F	S
	1	2	3	4	5	6
7	8	9	10	11	12	13
14	15	16	17	18	19	20
21	22	23	24	25	26	27
28	29	30	31			

March

LIGHTEN UP

Our need for excessive attention is that ego-centered part of us that says, "Look at me. I'm special. My story is more interesting than yours." It's that voice inside of us that may not come right out and say it, but that wants to believe that "my accomplishments are slightly more important than yours." The ego is that part of us that wants to be seen, heard, respected, considered special, often at the expense of someone else. To varying degrees, most of us engage in this habit, much to our own detriment.

February - March

SUNDAY 28

MONDAY 1

TUESDAY 2

WEDNESDAY 3

THURSDAY 4

FRIDAY 5

SATURDAY 6

FEBRUARY

S	M	T	W	T	F	S
	1	2	3	4	5	6
7	8	9	10	11	12	13
14	15	16	17	18	19	20
21	22	23	24	25	26	27
28						

APRIL

S	M	T	W	T	F	S
				1	2	3
4	5	6	7	8	9	10
11	12	13	14	15	16	17
18	19	20	21	22	23	24
25	26	27	28	29	30	

Without question, many of us have mastered the neurotic art of spending much of our lives worrying about a variety of things—all at once. We allow past problems and future concerns to dominate our present moments, so much so that we end up anxious, frustrated, depressed, and hopeless. On the flip side, we also postpone our gratification, our stated priorities, and our happiness, often convincing ourselves that "someday" will be better than today. Unfortunately, the same mental dynamics that tell us to look toward the future will only repeat themselves so that "someday" never actually arrives.

March

SUNDAY 7

MONDAY 8

TUESDAY 9

WEDNESDAY 10

THURSDAY 11

FRIDAY 12

SATURDAY 13

FEBRUARY

S	M	T	W	T	F	S
	1	2	3	4	5	6
7	8	9	10	11	12	13
14	15	16	17	18	19	20
21	22	23	24	25	26	27
28						

APRIL

S	M	T	W	T	F	S
				1	2	3
4	5	6	7	8	9	10
11	12	13	14	15	16	17
18	19	20	21	22	23	24
25	26	27	28	29	30	

A wonderful, heartfelt strategy for becoming more peaceful and loving is to practice allowing others the joy of being right—give them the glory. Stop correcting. As hard as it may be to change this habit, it's worth any effort and practice it takes.

March

SUNDAY 14

MONDAY 15

TUESDAY 16

WEDNESDAY 17

SAINT PATRICK'S DAY

THURSDAY 18

FRIDAY 19

SATURDAY 20

VERNAL EQUINOX

FEBRUARY

S	M	T	W	T	F	S
	1	2	3	4	5	6
7	8	9	10	11	12	13
14	15	16	17	18	19	20
21	22	23	24	25	26	27
28						

APRIL

S	M	T	W	T	F	S
				1	2	3
4	5	6	7	8	9	10
11	12	13	14	15	16	17
18	19	20	21	22	23	24
25	26	27	28	29	30	

The quality of patience goes a long way toward your goal of creating a more peaceful and loving self. The more patient you are, the more accepting you will be of what is, rather than insisting that life be exactly as you would like it to be. Without patience, life is extremely frustrating. You are easily annoyed, bothered, and irritated. Patience adds a dimension of ease and acceptance to your life. It's essential for inner peace.

March

SUNDAY 21

MONDAY 22

TUESDAY 23

WEDNESDAY 24

THURSDAY 25

FRIDAY 26

SATURDAY 27

FEBRUARY

S	M	T	W	T	F	S
	1	2	3	4	5	6
7	8	9	10	11	12	13
14	15	16	17	18	19	20
21	22	23	24	25	26	27
28						

APRIL

S	M	T	W	T	F	S
				1	2	3
4	5	6	7	8	9	10
11	12	13	14	15	16	17
18	19	20	21	22	23	24
25	26	27	28	29	30	

April

LET OTHERS HAVE THE GLORY

Whenever we hold on to our anger, we turn "small stuff" into really "big stuff" in our minds. We start to believe that our positions are more important than our happiness. They are not. If you want to be a more peaceful person you must understand that being right is almost never more important than allowing yourself to be happy. The way to be happy is to let go, and reach out. Let other people be right.

March - April

SUNDAY 28

MONDAY 29

TUESDAY 30

WEDNESDAY 31

THURSDAY 1

PASSOVER BEGINS

FRIDAY 2

GOOD FRIDAY

SATURDAY 3

MARCH

S	M	T	W	T	F	S
	1	2	3	4	5	6
7	8	9	10	11	12	13
14	15	16	17	18	19	20
21	22	23	24	25	26	27
28	29	30	31			

MAY

S	M	T	W	T	F	S
						1
2	3	4	5	6	7	8
9	10	11	12	13	14	15
16	17	18	19	20	21	22
23	24	25	26	27	28	29
30	31					

Whether it be an argument with your spouse, child, or boss, a mistake, a lost opportunity, a lost wallet, a work-related rejection, or a sprained ankle, chances are a year from now you aren't going to care. It will be one more irrelevant detail in your life. While this simple game won't solve all your problems, it can give you an enormous amount of needed perspective.

April

SUNDAY 4

DAYLIGHT SAVING TIME BEGINS
EASTER SUNDAY

MONDAY 5

EASTER MONDAY (CANADA)

TUESDAY 6

WEDNESDAY 7

THURSDAY 8

FRIDAY 9

PASSOVER ENDS

SATURDAY 10

MARCH

S	M	T	W	T	F	S
	1	2	3	4	5	6
7	8	9	10	11	12	13
14	15	16	17	18	19	20
21	22	23	24	25	26	27
28	29	30	31			

MAY

S	M	T	W	T	F	S
						1
2	3	4	5	6	7	8
9	10	11	12	13	14	15
16	17	18	19	20	21	22
23	24	25	26	27	28	29
30	31					

One of the mistakes many of us make is that we feel sorry for ourselves, or for others, thinking that life should be fair, or that someday it will be. It's not and it won't. When we make this mistake we tend to spend a lot of time wallowing and/or complaining about what's wrong with life. We commiserate with others, discussing the injustices of life. "It's not fair," we complain, not realizing that, perhaps, it was never intended to be.

April

SUNDAY 11

MONDAY 12

TUESDAY 13

WEDNESDAY 14

THURSDAY 15

FRIDAY 16

SATURDAY 17

MARCH

S	M	T	W	T	F	S
	1	2	3	4	5	6
7	8	9	10	11	12	13
14	15	16	17	18	19	20
21	22	23	24	25	26	27
28	29	30	31			

MAY

S	M	T	W	T	F	S
						1
2	3	4	5	6	7	8
9	10	11	12	13	14	15
16	17	18	19	20	21	22
23	24	25	26	27	28	29
30	31					

Much of our anxiety and inner struggle stems from our busy, overactive minds always needing something to entertain them, something to focus on, and always wondering "What's next?" While we're eating dinner we wonder what's for dessert. While eating dessert, we ponder what we should do afterward. After that evening, it's "What should we do this weekend?"

April

SUNDAY 18

MONDAY 19

PATRIOTS DAY

TUESDAY 20

WEDNESDAY 21

THURSDAY 22

EARTH DAY

FRIDAY 23

SATURDAY 24

MARCH

S	M	T	W	T	F	S
	1	2	3	4	5	6
7	8	9	10	11	12	13
14	15	16	17	18	19	20
21	22	23	24	25	26	27
28	29	30	31			

MAY

S	M	T	W	T	F	S
						1
2	3	4	5	6	7	8
9	10	11	12	13	14	15
16	17	18	19	20	21	22
23	24	25	26	27	28	29
30	31					

May

BE HAPPY WHERE YOU ARE

When you're feeling out of control and resentful of all you have to do, rather than roll up your sleeves and "get to it," a better strategy is to relax, take a few deep breaths, and go for a short walk. You'll find that when you catch yourself getting too stressed out—early, before it gets out of control—your stress will be like the proverbial snowball rolling down the hill. When it's small, it's manageable and easy to control. Once it gathers momentum, however, it's difficult, if not impossible, to stop.

April - May

SUNDAY 25

MONDAY 26

TUESDAY 27

WEDNESDAY 28

THURSDAY 29

TAKE OUR DAUGHTERS TO WORK DAY

FRIDAY 30

ARBOR DAY

SATURDAY 1

APRIL						
S	M	T	W	T	F	S
				1	2	3
4	5	6	7	8	9	10
11	12	13	14	15	16	17
18	19	20	21	22	23	24
25	26	27	28	29	30	

JUNE						
S	M	T	W	T	F	S
		1	2	3	4	5
6	7	8	9	10	11	12
13	14	15	16	17	18	19
20	21	22	23	24	25	26
27	28	29	30			

When we look back on our lives, how many of us are going to be pleased at how uptight we were? Almost universally, when people look back on their lives while on their deathbeds, they wish that their priorities had been quite different. With few exceptions, people wish they hadn't "sweated the small stuff" so much. Instead, they wish they had spent more time with the people and activities that they truly loved and less time worrying about aspects of life that, upon deeper examination, really don't matter all that much.

May

SUNDAY 2

MONDAY 3

TUESDAY 4

WEDNESDAY 5

THURSDAY 6

FRIDAY 7

SATURDAY 8

APRIL

S	M	T	W	T	F	S
				1	2	3
4	5	6	7	8	9	10
11	12	13	14	15	16	17
18	19	20	21	22	23	24
25	26	27	28	29	30	

JUNE

S	M	T	W	T	F	S
		1	2	3	4	5
6	7	8	9	10	11	12
13	14	15	16	17	18	19
20	21	22	23	24	25	26
27	28	29	30			

I've never met anyone (myself included) who hasn't turned little things into great big emergencies. We take our own goals so seriously that we forget to have fun along the way, and we forget to cut ourselves some slack. We take simple preferences and turn them into conditions for our own happiness.

May

SUNDAY 9

MOTHER'S DAY

MONDAY 10

TUESDAY 11

WEDNESDAY 12

THURSDAY 13

FRIDAY 14

SATURDAY 15

ARMED FORCES DAY

APRIL

S	M	T	W	T	F	S
				1	2	3
4	5	6	7	8	9	10
11	12	13	14	15	16	17
18	19	20	21	22	23	24
25	26	27	28	29	30	

JUNE

S	M	T	W	T	F	S
		1	2	3	4	5
6	7	8	9	10	11	12
13	14	15	16	17	18	19
20	21	22	23	24	25	26
27	28	29	30			

The back burner of your mind works in the same way as the back burner of a stove. While on low heat, the cooking process mixes, blends, and simmers the ingredients into a tasty meal. The way you prepared this meal was to throw the various ingredients into the pot, mix them up, and leave them alone. Often the less you interfere, the better the result.

May

SUNDAY 16

MONDAY 17

TUESDAY 18

WEDNESDAY 19

THURSDAY 20

FRIDAY 21

SATURDAY 22

APRIL

S	M	T	W	T	F	S
				1	2	3
4	5	6	7	8	9	10
11	12	13	14	15	16	17
18	19	20	21	22	23	24
25	26	27	28	29	30	

JUNE

S	M	T	W	T	F	S
		1	2	3	4	5
6	7	8	9	10	11	12
13	14	15	16	17	18	19
20	21	22	23	24	25	26
27	28	29	30			

Have you ever noticed or thought about how little eye contact most of us have with strangers? Why? Are we afraid of them? What keeps us from opening our hearts to people we don't know?

May

SUNDAY 23

MONDAY 24

VICTORIA DAY (CANADA)

TUESDAY 25

WEDNESDAY 26

THURSDAY 27

FRIDAY 28

SATURDAY 29

APRIL

S	M	T	W	T	F	S
				1	2	3
4	5	6	7	8	9	10
11	12	13	14	15	16	17
18	19	20	21	22	23	24
25	26	27	28	29	30	

JUNE

S	M	T	W	T	F	S
		1	2	3	4	5
6	7	8	9	10	11	12
13	14	15	16	17	18	19
20	21	22	23	24	25	26
27	28	29	30			

June

RELAX

Think of someone who truly irritates you, who makes you feel angry. Now, close your eyes and try to imagine this person as a tiny infant. Know that babies can't help but make mistakes and each of us was, at one time, a little infant. Now, roll forward the clock one hundred years. See the same person as a very old person who is about to die. Know that each of us will be one hundred years old, alive or dead, before too many decades go by.

May - June

SUNDAY 30

MEMORIAL DAY

MONDAY 31

MEMORIAL DAY (OBSERVED)

TUESDAY 1

WEDNESDAY 2

THURSDAY 3

FRIDAY 4

SATURDAY 5

MAY

S	M	T	W	T	F	S
						1
2	3	4	5	6	7	8
9	10	11	12	13	14	15
16	17	18	19	20	21	22
23	24	25	26	27	28	29
30	31					

JULY

S	M	T	W	T	F	S
				1	2	3
4	5	6	7	8	9	10
11	12	13	14	15	16	17
18	19	20	21	22	23	24
25	26	27	28	29	30	31

Essentially, "seek first to understand" implies that you become more interested in understanding others and less in having other people understand you. It means mastering the idea that if you want quality, fulfilling communication that is nourishing to you and others, understanding others must come first. When you understand where people are coming from, what they are trying to say, what's important to them, and so forth, being understood flows naturally; it falls into place with virtually no effort.

June

SUNDAY 6

MONDAY 7

TUESDAY 8

WEDNESDAY 9

THURSDAY 10

FRIDAY 11

SATURDAY 12

MAY

S	M	T	W	T	F	S
						1
2	3	4	5	6	7	8
9	10	11	12	13	14	15
16	17	18	19	20	21	22
23	24	25	26	27	28	29
30	31					

JULY

S	M	T	W	T	F	S
				1	2	3
4	5	6	7	8	9	10
11	12	13	14	15	16	17
18	19	20	21	22	23	24
25	26	27	28	29	30	31

Slowing down your responses and becoming a better listener aids you in becoming a more peaceful person. It takes pressure from you. If you think about it, you'll notice that it takes an enormous amount of energy and is very stressful to be sitting at the edge of your seat trying to guess what the person in front of you (or on the telephone) is going to say so that you can fire back your response.

June

SUNDAY 13

CHILDREN'S DAY

MONDAY 14

FLAG DAY

TUESDAY 15

WEDNESDAY 16

THURSDAY 17

FRIDAY 18

SATURDAY 19

MAY

S	M	T	W	T	F	S
						1
2	3	4	5	6	7	8
9	10	11	12	13	14	15
16	17	18	19	20	21	22
23	24	25	26	27	28	29
30	31					

JULY

S	M	T	W	T	F	S
				1	2	3
4	5	6	7	8	9	10
11	12	13	14	15	16	17
18	19	20	21	22	23	24
25	26	27	28	29	30	31

A more peaceful way to live is to decide consciously which battles are worth fighting and which are better left alone. If your primary goal isn't to have everything work out perfectly but instead to live a relatively stress-free life, you'll find that most battles pull you *away* from your most tranquil feelings. Is it really important that you prove to your spouse that you are right and she is wrong, or that you confront someone simply because it appears as though he or she has made a minor mistake?

June

SUNDAY **20**

FATHER'S DAY

MONDAY **21**

SUMMER SOLSTICE

TUESDAY **22**

WEDNESDAY **23**

THURSDAY **24**

FRIDAY **25**

SATURDAY **26**

MAY

S	M	T	W	T	F	S
						1
2	3	4	5	6	7	8
9	10	11	12	13	14	15
16	17	18	19	20	21	22
23	24	25	26	27	28	29
30	31					

JULY

S	M	T	W	T	F	S
				1	2	3
4	5	6	7	8	9	10
11	12	13	14	15	16	17
18	19	20	21	22	23	24
25	26	27	28	29	30	31

July

IMAGINE THAT EVERYONE IS ENLIGHTENED EXCEPT YOU

The truth is, life is almost never as bad as it seems when you're in a low mood. Rather than staying stuck in a bad temper, convinced you are seeing life realistically, you can learn to question your judgment. Remind yourself, "Of course I'm feeling defensive [or angry, frustrated, stressed, depressed]; I'm in a bad mood. I always feel negative when I'm low." When you're in an ill mood, learn to pass it off as simply that: an unavoidable human condition that will pass with time, if you leave it alone.

June - July

SUNDAY 27

MONDAY 28

TUESDAY 29

WEDNESDAY 30

THURSDAY 1

CANADA DAY

FRIDAY 2

SATURDAY 3

JUNE

S	M	T	W	T	F	S
		1	2	3	4	5
6	7	8	9	10	11	12
13	14	15	16	17	18	19
20	21	22	23	24	25	26
27	28	29	30			

AUGUST

S	M	T	W	T	F	S
1	2	3	4	5	6	7
8	9	10	11	12	13	14
15	16	17	18	19	20	21
22	23	24	25	26	27	28
29	30	31				

The sooner we accept the inevitable dilemma of not being able to win the approval of everyone we meet, the easier our lives will become. When you expect to be dished out your share of disapproval instead of struggling against this fact, you'll develop a helpful perspective to assist your life journey.

July

SUNDAY 4

INDEPENDENCE DAY

MONDAY 5

TUESDAY 6

WEDNESDAY 7

THURSDAY 8

FRIDAY 9

SATURDAY 10

JUNE

S	M	T	W	T	F	S
		1	2	3	4	5
6	7	8	9	10	11	12
13	14	15	16	17	18	19
20	21	22	23	24	25	26
27	28	29	30			

AUGUST

S	M	T	W	T	F	S
1	2	3	4	5	6	7
8	9	10	11	12	13	14
15	16	17	18	19	20	21
22	23	24	25	26	27	28
29	30	31				

Seeing the innocence is a powerful tool for transformation that means when someone is acting in a way that we don't like, the best strategy for dealing with that person is to distance ourselves from the behavior; to "look beyond it," so that we can see the innocence in where the behavior is coming from.

July

SUNDAY 11

MONDAY 12

TUESDAY 13

WEDNESDAY 14

THURSDAY 15

FRIDAY 16

SATURDAY 17

JUNE

S	M	T	W	T	F	S
		1	2	3	4	5
6	7	8	9	10	11	12
13	14	15	16	17	18	19
20	21	22	23	24	25	26
27	28	29	30			

AUGUST

S	M	T	W	T	F	S
1	2	3	4	5	6	7
8	9	10	11	12	13	14
15	16	17	18	19	20	21
22	23	24	25	26	27	28
29	30	31				

When your goal is to build people up, to make them feel better, to share in their joy, you too reap the rewards of their positive feelings. The next time you have the chance to correct someone, even if their facts are a little off, resist the temptation. Instead, ask yourself, "What do I really want out of this interaction?" Each time you resist "being right," and instead choose kindness, you'll notice a peaceful feeling within.

July

SUNDAY 18

MONDAY 19

TUESDAY 20

WEDNESDAY 21

THURSDAY 22

FRIDAY 23

SATURDAY 24

JUNE

S	M	T	W	T	F	S
		1	2	3	4	5
6	7	8	9	10	11	12
13	14	15	16	17	18	19
20	21	22	23	24	25	26
27	28	29	30			

AUGUST

S	M	T	W	T	F	S
1	2	3	4	5	6	7
8	9	10	11	12	13	14
15	16	17	18	19	20	21
22	23	24	25	26	27	28
29	30	31				

Proving yourself is a dangerous trap. It takes an enormous amount of energy to be continually pointing out your accomplishments, bragging, or trying to convince others of your worth as a human being. Bragging actually dilutes the positive feelings you receive from an accomplishment or something you are proud of.

July

SUNDAY 25

MONDAY 26

TUESDAY 27

WEDNESDAY 28

THURSDAY 29

FRIDAY 30

SATURDAY 31

JUNE

S	M	T	W	T	F	S
		1	2	3	4	5
6	7	8	9	10	11	12
13	14	15	16	17	18	19
20	21	22	23	24	25	26
27	28	29	30			

AUGUST

S	M	T	W	T	F	S
1	2	3	4	5	6	7
8	9	10	11	12	13	14
15	16	17	18	19	20	21
22	23	24	25	26	27	28
29	30	31				

August

SEE THE INNOCENCE

It's really difficult to become a contented person if you're keeping score of all you do. Keeping track only discourages you by cluttering your mind with who's doing what, who's doing more, and so forth. If you want to know the truth about it, this is the epitome of "small stuff."

August

SUNDAY 1

MONDAY 2

Civic Holiday (Canada)

TUESDAY 3

WEDNESDAY 4

THURSDAY 5

FRIDAY 6

SATURDAY 7

JULY

S	M	T	W	T	F	S
				1	2	3
4	5	6	7	8	9	10
11	12	13	14	15	16	17
18	19	20	21	22	23	24
25	26	27	28	29	30	31

SEPTEMBER

S	M	T	W	T	F	S
			1	2	3	4
5	6	7	8	9	10	11
12	13	14	15	16	17	18
19	20	21	22	23	24	25
26	27	28	29	30		

When someone acts in a way that seems strange to you, rather than reacting in your usual way, such as, "I can't believe they would do that," instead say something to yourself like "I see, that must be the way she sees things in her world. Very interesting."

August

SUNDAY 8

MONDAY 9

TUESDAY 10

WEDNESDAY 11

THURSDAY 12

FRIDAY 13

SATURDAY 14

JULY

S	M	T	W	T	F	S
				1	2	3
4	5	6	7	8	9	10
11	12	13	14	15	16	17
18	19	20	21	22	23	24
25	26	27	28	29	30	31

SEPTEMBER

S	M	T	W	T	F	S
			1	2	3	4
5	6	7	8	9	10	11
12	13	14	15	16	17	18
19	20	21	22	23	24	25
26	27	28	29	30		

Telling someone something that you like, admire, or appreciate about them is a "random act of kindness." It takes almost no effort (once you get used to it), yet it pays enormous dividends. Many people spend their entire lifetimes wishing that other people would acknowledge them.

August

SUNDAY 15

MONDAY 16

TUESDAY 17

WEDNESDAY 18

THURSDAY 19

FRIDAY 20

SATURDAY 21

JULY

S	M	T	W	T	F	S
				1	2	3
4	5	6	7	8	9	10
11	12	13	14	15	16	17
18	19	20	21	22	23	24
25	26	27	28	29	30	31

SEPTEMBER

S	M	T	W	T	F	S
			1	2	3	4
5	6	7	8	9	10	11
12	13	14	15	16	17	18
19	20	21	22	23	24	25
26	27	28	29	30		

When our life is filled with the desire to see the holiness in everyday things, something magical begins to happen. A feeling of peace emerges. We begin to see nurturing aspects of daily living that were previously hidden to us. When we remember that everything has God's fingerprints on it, that alone makes it special.

August

SUNDAY 22

MONDAY 23

TUESDAY 24

WEDNESDAY 25

THURSDAY 26

FRIDAY 27

SATURDAY 28

JULY

S	M	T	W	T	F	S
				1	2	3
4	5	6	7	8	9	10
11	12	13	14	15	16	17
18	19	20	21	22	23	24
25	26	27	28	29	30	31

SEPTEMBER

S	M	T	W	T	F	S
			1	2	3	4
5	6	7	8	9	10	11
12	13	14	15	16	17	18
19	20	21	22	23	24	25
26	27	28	29	30		

September

PRACTICE BEING IN THE "EYE OF THE STORM"

If you take a moment to observe how you actually feel immediately after you criticize someone, you'll notice that you will feel a little deflated and ashamed, almost like *you're* the one who has been attacked. The reason this is true is that when we criticize, it's a statement to the world and to ourselves, "I have a need to be critical."

August - September

SUNDAY 29

MONDAY 30

TUESDAY 31

WEDNESDAY 1

THURSDAY 2

FRIDAY 3

SATURDAY 4

AUGUST

S	M	T	W	T	F	S
1	2	3	4	5	6	7
8	9	10	11	12	13	14
15	16	17	18	19	20	21
22	23	24	25	26	27	28
29	30	31				

OCTOBER

S	M	T	W	T	F	S
					1	2
3	4	5	6	7	8	9
10	11	12	13	14	15	16
17	18	19	20	21	22	23
24	25	26	27	28	29	30
31						

Almost every opinion has some merit, especially if we are looking for merit, rather than looking for errors. The next time someone offers you an opinion, rather than judge or criticize it, see if you can find a grain of truth in what the person is saying.

September

SUNDAY 5

MONDAY 6

LABOR DAY

TUESDAY 7

WEDNESDAY 8

THURSDAY 9

FRIDAY 10

SATURDAY 11

ROSH HASHANAH

AUGUST

S	M	T	W	T	F	S
1	2	3	4	5	6	7
8	9	10	11	12	13	14
15	16	17	18	19	20	21
22	23	24	25	26	27	28
29	30	31				

OCTOBER

S	M	T	W	T	F	S
					1	2
3	4	5	6	7	8	9
10	11	12	13	14	15	16
17	18	19	20	21	22	23
24	25	26	27	28	29	30
31						

When you observe peaceful, relaxed people, you find that when they are feeling good, they are very grateful. They understand that both positive and negative feelings come and go, and that there will come a time when they won't be feeling so good.

September

SUNDAY 12

GRANDPARENTS' DAY

MONDAY 13

TUESDAY 14

WEDNESDAY 15

THURSDAY 16

FRIDAY 17

SATURDAY 18

AUGUST

S	M	T	W	T	F	S
1	2	3	4	5	6	7
8	9	10	11	12	13	14
15	16	17	18	19	20	21
22	23	24	25	26	27	28
29	30	31				

OCTOBER

S	M	T	W	T	F	S
					1	2
3	4	5	6	7	8	9
10	11	12	13	14	15	16
17	18	19	20	21	22	23
24	25	26	27	28	29	30
31						

It's useful to think of relaxation as a quality of heart that you can access on a regular basis rather than something reserved for some later time. You can relax now. It's helpful to remember that relaxed people can still be superachievers and, in fact, that relaxation and creativity go hand in hand.

September

SUNDAY 19

MONDAY 20

YOM KIPPUR

TUESDAY 21

WEDNESDAY 22

THURSDAY 23

AUTUMNAL EQUINOX

FRIDAY 24

SATURDAY 25

AUGUST

S	M	T	W	T	F	S
1	2	3	4	5	6	7
8	9	10	11	12	13	14
15	16	17	18	19	20	21
22	23	24	25	26	27	28
29	30	31				

OCTOBER

S	M	T	W	T	F	S
					1	2
3	4	5	6	7	8	9
10	11	12	13	14	15	16
17	18	19	20	21	22	23
24	25	26	27	28	29	30
31						

October

UNDERSTAND SEPARATE REALITIES

When you do too many things at once, it's impossible to be present-moment oriented. Thus, you not only lose out on much of the potential enjoyment of what you are doing, but you also become far less focused and effective.

September - October

SUNDAY 26

MONDAY 27

TUESDAY 28

WEDNESDAY 29

THURSDAY 30

FRIDAY 1

SATURDAY 2

SEPTEMBER

S	M	T	W	T	F	S
			1	2	3	4
5	6	7	8	9	10	11
12	13	14	15	16	17	18
19	20	21	22	23	24	25
26	27	28	29	30		

NOVEMBER

S	M	T	W	T	F	S
	1	2	3	4	5	6
7	8	9	10	11	12	13
14	15	16	17	18	19	20
21	22	23	24	25	26	27
28	29	30				

We often use the excuse that it's natural to be frustrated when our plans change. That depends, however, on what your priorities are. Is it more important to stick to some rigid writing schedule or to be available to my four-year-old? The more general question is, "What's more important, getting what I want and keeping my plans, or learning to go with the flow?"

October

SUNDAY 3

MONDAY 4

TUESDAY 5

WEDNESDAY 6

THURSDAY 7

FRIDAY 8

SATURDAY 9

SEPTEMBER

S	M	T	W	T	F	S
			1	2	3	4
5	6	7	8	9	10	11
12	13	14	15	16	17	18
19	20	21	22	23	24	25
26	27	28	29	30		

NOVEMBER

S	M	T	W	T	F	S
	1	2	3	4	5	6
7	8	9	10	11	12	13
14	15	16	17	18	19	20
21	22	23	24	25	26	27
28	29	30				

In a practical sense, you really have only two options when it comes to dealing with negative thoughts. You can analyze your thoughts—ponder, think through, study, think some more—or you can learn to ignore them—dismiss, pay less attention to, not take so seriously. This latter option, learning to take your negative thoughts less seriously, is infinitely more effective in terms of learning to be more peaceful.

October

SUNDAY 10

MONDAY 11

THANKSGIVING DAY (CANADA)
COLUMBUS DAY (OBSERVED)

TUESDAY 12

WEDNESDAY 13

THURSDAY 14

FRIDAY 15

SATURDAY 16

SEPTEMBER

S	M	T	W	T	F	S
			1	2	3	4
5	6	7	8	9	10	11
12	13	14	15	16	17	18
19	20	21	22	23	24	25
26	27	28	29	30		

NOVEMBER

S	M	T	W	T	F	S
	1	2	3	4	5	6
7	8	9	10	11	12	13
14	15	16	17	18	19	20
21	22	23	24	25	26	27
28	29	30				

Although there are many techniques for quieting the mind, such as reflection, deep breathing, contemplation, and visualization, the most universally accepted and regularly used technique is meditation. In as little as five to ten minutes a day, you can train your mind to be still and quiet.

October

SUNDAY 17

MONDAY 18

TUESDAY 19

WEDNESDAY 20

THURSDAY 21

FRIDAY 22

SATURDAY 23

SEPTEMBER

S	M	T	W	T	F	S
			1	2	3	4
5	6	7	8	9	10	11
12	13	14	15	16	17	18
19	20	21	22	23	24	25
26	27	28	29	30		

NOVEMBER

S	M	T	W	T	F	S
	1	2	3	4	5	6
7	8	9	10	11	12	13
14	15	16	17	18	19	20
21	22	23	24	25	26	27
28	29	30				

Although yoga is physical in nature, its benefits are both physical and emotional. On the physical side, yoga strengthens the muscles and the spine, creating flexibility and ease of motion. On the emotional side, yoga is a tremendous stress reducer. It balances the body-mind-spirit connection, giving you a feeling of ease and peace.

October

SUNDAY 24

UNITED NATIONS DAY

MONDAY 25

TUESDAY 26

WEDNESDAY 27

THURSDAY 28

FRIDAY 29

SATURDAY 30

SEPTEMBER

S	M	T	W	T	F	S
			1	2	3	4
5	6	7	8	9	10	11
12	13	14	15	16	17	18
19	20	21	22	23	24	25
26	27	28	29	30		

NOVEMBER

S	M	T	W	T	F	S
	1	2	3	4	5	6
7	8	9	10	11	12	13
14	15	16	17	18	19	20
21	22	23	24	25	26	27
28	29	30				

November

UNDERSTAND THE STATEMENT,
"WHEREVER YOU GO, THERE YOU ARE"

When you do something nice for someone, just to do it, you'll notice (if you're quiet enough inside yourself) a beautiful feeling of ease and peace. Just as vigorous exercise releases endorphins in your brain that make you feel good physically, your acts of loving-kindness release the emotional equivalent.

October - November

SUNDAY 31

DAYLIGHT SAVING TIME ENDS
HALLOWEEN

MONDAY 1

TUESDAY 2

ELECTION DAY

WEDNESDAY 3

THURSDAY 4

FRIDAY 5

SATURDAY 6

OCTOBER

S	M	T	W	T	F	S
					1	2
3	4	5	6	7	8	9
10	11	12	13	14	15	16
17	18	19	20	21	22	23
24	25	26	27	28	29	30
31						

DECEMBER

S	M	T	W	T	F	S
			1	2	3	4
5	6	7	8	9	10	11
12	13	14	15	16	17	18
19	20	21	22	23	24	25
26	27	28	29	30	31	

One of the reasons it's important to accept all aspects of yourself is that it allows you to be easier on yourself, more compassionate. When you act or feel insecure, rather than pretending to be "together," you can open to the truth and say to yourself, "I'm feeling frightened and that's okay." If you're feeling a little jealous, greedy, or angry, rather than deny or bury your feelings, you can open to them, which helps you move through them quickly and grow beyond them.

November

SUNDAY 7

MONDAY 8

TUESDAY 9

WEDNESDAY 10

THURSDAY 11

REMEMBRANCE DAY (CANADA)
VETERANS DAY

FRIDAY 12

SATURDAY 13

OCTOBER

S	M	T	W	T	F	S
					1	2
3	4	5	6	7	8	9
10	11	12	13	14	15	16
17	18	19	20	21	22	23
24	25	26	27	28	29	30
31						

DECEMBER

S	M	T	W	T	F	S
			1	2	3	4
5	6	7	8	9	10	11
12	13	14	15	16	17	18
19	20	21	22	23	24	25
26	27	28	29	30	31	

In terms of personal happiness, you cannot be peaceful while at the same time blaming others. Surely there are times when other people and/or circumstances contribute to our problems, but it is we who must rise to the occasion and take responsibility for our own happiness. Circumstances don't make a person, they reveal him or her.

November

SUNDAY 14

MONDAY 15

TUESDAY 16

WEDNESDAY 17

THURSDAY 18

FRIDAY 19

SATURDAY 20

OCTOBER

S	M	T	W	T	F	S
					1	2
3	4	5	6	7	8	9
10	11	12	13	14	15	16
17	18	19	20	21	22	23
24	25	26	27	28	29	30
31						

DECEMBER

S	M	T	W	T	F	S
			1	2	3	4
5	6	7	8	9	10	11
12	13	14	15	16	17	18
19	20	21	22	23	24	25
26	27	28	29	30	31	

The root of being uptight is our unwillingness to accept life as being different, in any way, from our expectations. Very simply, we want things to be a certain way but they're not a certain way. Life is simply as it is.

November

SUNDAY 21

MONDAY 22

TUESDAY 23

WEDNESDAY 24

THURSDAY 25

THANKSGIVING DAY

FRIDAY 26

SATURDAY 27

OCTOBER

S	M	T	W	T	F	S
					1	2
3	4	5	6	7	8	9
10	11	12	13	14	15	16
17	18	19	20	21	22	23
24	25	26	27	28	29	30
31						

DECEMBER

S	M	T	W	T	F	S
			1	2	3	4
5	6	7	8	9	10	11
12	13	14	15	16	17	18
19	20	21	22	23	24	25
26	27	28	29	30	31	

December

QUIET THE MIND

When your experience of life is other than pleasant—when you're feeling angry, resentful, depressed, stressed out, frustrated, and so forth, your warning system of feelings kicks in like a red flag to remind you that you are off track, that it's time to ease up on your thinking, you've lost perspective. Mental adjustment needs to be made.

November - December

SUNDAY 28

MONDAY 29

TUESDAY 30

WEDNESDAY 1

THURSDAY 2

FRIDAY 3

SATURDAY 4

Hanukkah

NOVEMBER

S	M	T	W	T	F	S
	1	2	3	4	5	6
7	8	9	10	11	12	13
14	15	16	17	18	19	20
21	22	23	24	25	26	27
28	29	30				

JANUARY

S	M	T	W	T	F	S
						1
2	3	4	5	6	7	8
9	10	11	12	13	14	15
16	17	18	19	20	21	22
23	24	25	26	27	28	29
30	31					

It has been said that "the shortest distance between two points is an intention." This is certainly true with regard to a life filled with love. The starting point or foundation of a life filled with love is the desire and commitment to be a source of love. Our attitude, choices, acts of kindness, and willingness to be the first to reach out will take us toward this goal.

December

SUNDAY 5

MONDAY 6

TUESDAY 7

WEDNESDAY 8

THURSDAY 9

RAMADAN

FRIDAY 10

SATURDAY 11

NOVEMBER

S	M	T	W	T	F	S
	1	2	3	4	5	6
7	8	9	10	11	12	13
14	15	16	17	18	19	20
21	22	23	24	25	26	27
28	29	30				

JANUARY

S	M	T	W	T	F	S
						1
2	3	4	5	6	7	8
9	10	11	12	13	14	15
16	17	18	19	20	21	22
23	24	25	26	27	28	29
30	31					

Trusting your intuitive heart means listening to and trusting that quiet inner voice that knows what it is you need to do, what actions need to be taken, or changes need to be made in your life. Many of us don't listen to our intuitive heart for fear that we couldn't possibly know something without thinking it through, or for fear that legitimate answers could possibly be so obvious.

December

SUNDAY 12

MONDAY 13

TUESDAY 14

WEDNESDAY 15

THURSDAY 16

FRIDAY 17

SATURDAY 18

NOVEMBER

S	M	T	W	T	F	S
	1	2	3	4	5	6
7	8	9	10	11	12	13
14	15	16	17	18	19	20
21	22	23	24	25	26	27
28	29	30				

JANUARY

S	M	T	W	T	F	S
						1
2	3	4	5	6	7	8
9	10	11	12	13	14	15
16	17	18	19	20	21	22
23	24	25	26	27	28	29
30	31					

If you can learn to open your heart in the midst of the difficulties of daily life, you will soon find that many of the things that have always bothered you will cease to be concerns. Your perspective will deepen. When you fight that which you struggle with, life can be quite a battle, almost like a Ping-Pong game where you are the ball. But when you surrender to the moment, accept what is going on, make it okay, more peaceful feelings will begin to emerge.

December

SUNDAY 19

MONDAY 20

TUESDAY 21

WEDNESDAY 22

THURSDAY 23

FRIDAY 24

SATURDAY 25

CHRISTMAS

NOVEMBER

S	M	T	W	T	F	S
	1	2	3	4	5	6
7	8	9	10	11	12	13
14	15	16	17	18	19	20
21	22	23	24	25	26	27
28	29	30				

JANUARY

S	M	T	W	T	F	S
						1
2	3	4	5	6	7	8
9	10	11	12	13	14	15
16	17	18	19	20	21	22
23	24	25	26	27	28	29
30	31					

When are you going to die? In fifty years, twenty, ten, five, today? Last time I checked, no one had told me. The truth is, none of us has any idea how long we have to live. Sadly, however, we act as if we're going to live forever. Instead, we should live each day as if it is our last.

December

SUNDAY 26

KWANZAA
BOXING DAY (CANADA)

MONDAY 27

TUESDAY 28

WEDNESDAY 29

THURSDAY 30

FRIDAY 31

SATURDAY 1

NOVEMBER

S	M	T	W	T	F	S
	1	2	3	4	5	6
7	8	9	10	11	12	13
14	15	16	17	18	19	20
21	22	23	24	25	26	27
28	29	30				

JANUARY

S	M	T	W	T	F	S
						1
2	3	4	5	6	7	8
9	10	11	12	13	14	15
16	17	18	19	20	21	22
23	24	25	26	27	28	29
30	31					

January

SUNDAY 2

MONDAY 3

TUESDAY 4

WEDNESDAY 5

THURSDAY 6

FRIDAY 7

SATURDAY 8

DECEMBER

S	M	T	W	T	F	S
			1	2	3	4
5	6	7	8	9	10	11
12	13	14	15	16	17	18
19	20	21	22	23	24	25
26	27	28	29	30	31	

FEBRUARY

S	M	T	W	T	F	S
		1	2	3	4	5
6	7	8	9	10	11	12
13	14	15	16	17	18	19
20	21	22	23	24	25	26
27	28	29				

1998 Calendar

JANUARY

S	M	T	W	T	F	S
				1	2	3
4	5	6	7	8	9	10
11	12	13	14	15	16	17
18	19	20	21	22	23	24
25	26	27	28	29	30	31

FEBRUARY

S	M	T	W	T	F	S
1	2	3	4	5	6	7
8	9	10	11	12	13	14
15	16	17	18	19	20	21
22	23	24	25	26	27	28

MARCH

S	M	T	W	T	F	S
1	2	3	4	5	6	7
8	9	10	11	12	13	14
15	16	17	18	19	20	21
22	23	24	25	26	27	28
29	30	31				

APRIL

S	M	T	W	T	F	S
			1	2	3	4
5	6	7	8	9	10	11
12	13	14	15	16	17	18
19	20	21	22	23	24	25
26	27	28	29	30		

MAY

S	M	T	W	T	F	S
					1	2
3	4	5	6	7	8	9
10	11	12	13	14	15	16
17	18	19	20	21	22	23
24	25	26	27	28	29	30
31						

JUNE

S	M	T	W	T	F	S
	1	2	3	4	5	6
7	8	9	10	11	12	13
14	15	16	17	18	19	20
21	22	23	24	25	26	27
28	29	30				

JULY

S	M	T	W	T	F	S
			1	2	3	4
5	6	7	8	9	10	11
12	13	14	15	16	17	18
19	20	21	22	23	24	25
26	27	28	29	30	31	

AUGUST

S	M	T	W	T	F	S
						1
2	3	4	5	6	7	8
9	10	11	12	13	14	15
16	17	18	19	20	21	22
23	24	25	26	27	28	29
30	31					

SEPTEMBER

S	M	T	W	T	F	S
		1	2	3	4	5
6	7	8	9	10	11	12
13	14	15	16	17	18	19
20	21	22	23	24	25	26
27	28	29	30			

OCTOBER

S	M	T	W	T	F	S
				1	2	3
4	5	6	7	8	9	10
11	12	13	14	15	16	17
18	19	20	21	22	23	24
25	26	27	28	29	30	31

NOVEMBER

S	M	T	W	T	F	S
1	2	3	4	5	6	7
8	9	10	11	12	13	14
15	16	17	18	19	20	21
22	23	24	25	26	27	28
29	30					

DECEMBER

S	M	T	W	T	F	S
		1	2	3	4	5
6	7	8	9	10	11	12
13	14	15	16	17	18	19
20	21	22	23	24	25	26
27	28	29	30	31		

1999 Calendar

JANUARY

S	M	T	W	T	F	S
					1	2
3	4	5	6	7	8	9
10	11	12	13	14	15	16
17	18	19	20	21	22	23
24	25	26	27	28	29	30
31						

FEBRUARY

S	M	T	W	T	F	S
	1	2	3	4	5	6
7	8	9	10	11	12	13
14	15	16	17	18	19	20
21	22	23	24	25	26	27
28						

MARCH

S	M	T	W	T	F	S
	1	2	3	4	5	6
7	8	9	10	11	12	13
14	15	16	17	18	19	20
21	22	23	24	25	26	27
28	29	30	31			

APRIL

S	M	T	W	T	F	S
				1	2	3
4	5	6	7	8	9	10
11	12	13	14	15	16	17
18	19	20	21	22	23	24
25	26	27	28	29	30	

MAY

S	M	T	W	T	F	S
						1
2	3	4	5	6	7	8
9	10	11	12	13	14	15
16	17	18	19	20	21	22
23	24	25	26	27	28	29
30	31					

JUNE

S	M	T	W	T	F	S
		1	2	3	4	5
6	7	8	9	10	11	12
13	14	15	16	17	18	19
20	21	22	23	24	25	26
27	28	29	30			

JULY

S	M	T	W	T	F	S
				1	2	3
4	5	6	7	8	9	10
11	12	13	14	15	16	17
18	19	20	21	22	23	24
25	26	27	28	29	30	31

AUGUST

S	M	T	W	T	F	S
1	2	3	4	5	6	7
8	9	10	11	12	13	14
15	16	17	18	19	20	21
22	23	24	25	26	27	28
29	30	31				

SEPTEMBER

S	M	T	W	T	F	S
			1	2	3	4
5	6	7	8	9	10	11
12	13	14	15	16	17	18
19	20	21	22	23	24	25
26	27	28	29	30		

OCTOBER

S	M	T	W	T	F	S
					1	2
3	4	5	6	7	8	9
10	11	12	13	14	15	16
17	18	19	20	21	22	23
24	25	26	27	28	29	30
31						

NOVEMBER

S	M	T	W	T	F	S
	1	2	3	4	5	6
7	8	9	10	11	12	13
14	15	16	17	18	19	20
21	22	23	24	25	26	27
28	29	30				

DECEMBER

S	M	T	W	T	F	S
			1	2	3	4
5	6	7	8	9	10	11
12	13	14	15	16	17	18
19	20	21	22	23	24	25
26	27	28	29	30	31	

2000 Calendar

JANUARY

S	M	T	W	T	F	S
						1
2	3	4	5	6	7	8
9	10	11	12	13	14	15
16	17	18	19	20	21	22
23	24	25	26	27	28	29
30	31					

FEBRUARY

S	M	T	W	T	F	S
		1	2	3	4	5
6	7	8	9	10	11	12
13	14	15	16	17	18	19
20	21	22	23	24	25	26
27	28	29				

MARCH

S	M	T	W	T	F	S
			1	2	3	4
5	6	7	8	9	10	11
12	13	14	15	16	17	18
19	20	21	22	23	24	25
26	27	28	29	30	31	

APRIL

S	M	T	W	T	F	S
						1
2	3	4	5	6	7	8
9	10	11	12	13	14	15
16	17	18	19	20	21	22
23	24	25	26	27	28	29
30						

MAY

S	M	T	W	T	F	S
	1	2	3	4	5	6
7	8	9	10	11	12	13
14	15	16	17	18	19	20
21	22	23	24	25	26	27
28	29	30	31			

JUNE

S	M	T	W	T	F	S
				1	2	3
4	5	6	7	8	9	10
11	12	13	14	15	16	17
18	19	20	21	22	23	24
25	26	27	28	29	30	

JULY

S	M	T	W	T	F	S
						1
2	3	4	5	6	7	8
9	10	11	12	13	14	15
16	17	18	19	20	21	22
23	24	25	26	27	28	29
30	31					

AUGUST

S	M	T	W	T	F	S
		1	2	3	4	5
6	7	8	9	10	11	12
13	14	15	16	17	18	19
20	21	22	23	24	25	26
27	28	29	30	31		

SEPTEMBER

S	M	T	W	T	F	S
					1	2
3	4	5	6	7	8	9
10	11	12	13	14	15	16
17	18	19	20	21	22	23
24	25	26	27	28	29	30

OCTOBER

S	M	T	W	T	F	S
1	2	3	4	5	6	7
8	9	10	11	12	13	14
15	16	17	18	19	20	21
22	23	24	25	26	27	28
29	30	31				

NOVEMBER

S	M	T	W	T	F	S
			1	2	3	4
5	6	7	8	9	10	11
12	13	14	15	16	17	18
19	20	21	22	23	24	25
26	27	28	29	30		

DECEMBER

S	M	T	W	T	F	S
					1	2
3	4	5	6	7	8	9
10	11	12	13	14	15	16
17	18	19	20	21	22	23
24	25	26	27	28	29	30
31						

2001 Calendar

JANUARY

S	M	T	W	T	F	S
	1	2	3	4	5	6
7	8	9	10	11	12	13
14	15	16	17	18	19	20
21	22	23	24	25	26	27
28	29	30	31			

FEBRUARY

S	M	T	W	T	F	S
				1	2	3
4	5	6	7	8	9	10
11	12	13	14	15	16	17
18	19	20	21	22	23	24
25	26	27	28			

MARCH

S	M	T	W	T	F	S
				1	2	3
4	5	6	7	8	9	10
11	12	13	14	15	16	17
18	19	20	21	22	23	24
25	26	27	28	29	30	31

APRIL

S	M	T	W	T	F	S
1	2	3	4	5	6	7
8	9	10	11	12	13	14
15	16	17	18	19	20	21
22	23	24	25	26	27	28
29	30					

MAY

S	M	T	W	T	F	S
		1	2	3	4	5
6	7	8	9	10	11	12
13	14	15	16	17	18	19
20	21	22	23	24	25	26
27	28	29	30	31		

JUNE

S	M	T	W	T	F	S
					1	2
3	4	5	6	7	8	9
10	11	12	13	14	15	16
17	18	19	20	21	22	23
24	25	26	27	28	29	30

JULY

S	M	T	W	T	F	S
1	2	3	4	5	6	7
8	9	10	11	12	13	14
15	16	17	18	19	20	21
22	23	24	25	26	27	28
29	30	31				

AUGUST

S	M	T	W	T	F	S
			1	2	3	4
5	6	7	8	9	10	11
12	13	14	15	16	17	18
19	20	21	22	23	24	25
26	27	28	29	30	31	

SEPTEMBER

S	M	T	W	T	F	S
						1
2	3	4	5	6	7	8
9	10	11	12	13	14	15
16	17	18	19	20	21	22
23	24	25	26	27	28	29
30						

OCTOBER

S	M	T	W	T	F	S
	1	2	3	4	5	6
7	8	9	10	11	12	13
14	15	16	17	18	19	20
21	22	23	24	25	26	27
28	29	30	31			

NOVEMBER

S	M	T	W	T	F	S
				1	2	3
4	5	6	7	8	9	10
11	12	13	14	15	16	17
18	19	20	21	22	23	24
25	26	27	28	29	30	

DECEMBER

S	M	T	W	T	F	S
						1
2	3	4	5	6	7	8
9	10	11	12	13	14	15
16	17	18	19	20	21	22
23	24	25	26	27	28	29
30	31					

Notes

Notes

Notes

Notes

Notes